Foster Care 101: Insights and Tips for New and Existing Foster Parents

Navigating Your Journey With Confidence

Tanya Orr

© **Copyright 2024 - All rights reserved.**

The content contained within this book may not be reproduced, duplicated or transmitted without direct written permission from the author or the publisher.

Under no circumstances will any blame or legal responsibility be held against the publisher, or author, for any damages, reparation, or monetary loss due to the information contained within this book, either directly or indirectly.

Legal Notice:

This book is copyright protected. It is only for personal use. You cannot amend, distribute, sell, use, quote or paraphrase any part, or the content within this book, without the consent of the author or publisher.

Disclaimer Notice:

Please note the information contained within this document is for educational and entertainment purposes only. All effort has been executed to present accurate, up to date, reliable, complete information. No warranties of any kind are declared or implied. Readers acknowledge that the author is not engaged in the rendering of legal, financial, medical or professional advice. The content within this book has been derived from various sources. Please consult a licensed professional before attempting any techniques outlined in this book.

By reading this document, the reader agrees that under no circumstances is the author responsible for any losses, direct or indirect, that are incurred as a result of the use of the information contained within this document, including, but not limited to, errors, omissions, or inaccuracies.

Table of Contents

INTRODUCTION 1

CHAPTER 1: INTRODUCTION TO FOSTER CARE 3
    WHAT IS CPS? 4
        How CPS Identifies Children in Need 4
        Why Children Enter Foster Care 5
    STATISTICS ON FOSTER CARE 7
        Implications of These Statistics 7
    THE DIFFERENCE BETWEEN ADOPTION AND FOSTER CARE 8
        Definitions and Long-Term Goals 8
        Legal Differences and Permanency 8
        Misconceptions of Foster Care 9

CHAPTER 2: THE EMOTIONAL JOURNEY: UNDERSTANDING THE CHILD'S PERSPECTIVE 11
    TRAUMA AND ITS EFFECTS ON CHILDREN 12
        Psychological Impacts of Trauma 12
        The Physical Manifestation of Traumatic Stress 13
    RECOGNIZING SIGNS OF PAST ABUSE OR NEGLECT 14
        Physical Signs 15
        Emotional Signs 15
    ATTACHMENT AND TRUST-BUILDING 17
        Importance of Secure Attachments 17
    THE IMPORTANCE OF PATIENCE AND UNDERSTANDING 18
    STRATEGIES TO CULTIVATE TRUST 19

CHAPTER 3: PREPARING YOUR HOME AND HEART 21
    HOME STUDY AND SAFETY REQUIREMENTS 22
        What Is a Home Study? 22
        Training and Interviews 23
        A Home Visit 23
        Background Checks 24
        Medical Reports and Financial Statements 24
        References 25
    PREPARING FOR THE HOME STUDY 25
        Openness and Feedback 26
        Adjusting Your Family Dynamics 26

Involving Your Own Children 26
PREPARING FOR CHANGE 28
Set Clear Expectations 28
Prioritize Family Time 29
FINANCIAL AND LEGAL PREPARATIONS 29
Legal Protections and Rights 29
EMOTIONAL READINESS 30

CHAPTER 4: THE FIRST DAYS: BUILDING A SAFE HAVEN 33

WELCOMING A CHILD TO YOUR HOME 34
Welcoming Ideas 34
Home Tour and Safety Overview 35
Setting Boundaries, Routines, and Expectations 35
BUILDING BONDS 36
UNDERSTANDING AND MANAGING INITIAL BEHAVIORS 37
Early Behavioral Challenges 37
Strategies for Behavioral Challenges 38

CHAPTER 5: NAVIGATING RELATIONSHIPS: BIRTH FAMILIES AND CASEWORKERS 41

THE IMPORTANCE OF MAINTAINING BIRTH FAMILY CONNECTIONS 42
The Role of Birth Families in a Child's Life 42
Navigating the Challenges 42
Importance of Siblings 44
Tips for Bonding Moments 44
THE ROLE OF THE CASEWORKER IN YOUR FOSTER JOURNEY 45
Understanding the Caseworker's Responsibilities 45
Build a Collaborative Relationship 46
NAVIGATING DISAGREEMENTS AND CONFLICTS 47

CHAPTER 6: EDUCATIONAL AND DEVELOPMENTAL GAP CHALLENGES 49

ADDRESSING EDUCATIONAL GAPS 49
Legal Rights and Involvements 50
Recognizing the Signs 51
STRATEGIES TO BRIDGE THE GAPS 52
SUPPORTING SPECIAL EDUCATION NEEDS 53
Strategies for Support 53
Home Environment 54
THE IMPORTANCE OF LIFE SKILLS 55

CHAPTER 7: CELEBRATING MILESTONES AND CREATING MEMORIES 57

RECOGNIZING SMALL WINS 57
The Power of Positive Reinforcement 57
Celebrating Growth and Resilience 58

ENCOURAGING THE CHILD'S PASSIONS AND TALENTS 60
   Identifying Strengths and Interests.. 60
   Nurture Strengths and Support Exploration 61
   Applaud Efforts and Encourage Authenticity.. 62
   Resources and Activities for Enrichment... 62
BUILDING TRADITIONS AND CREATING LASTING BONDS 63
   Ideas for Traditions 64

CHAPTER 8: SUPPORTING TRANSITIONS: REUNIFICATION OR ADOPTION 67

THE EMOTIONAL COMPLEXITY OF REUNIFICATION 67
   Understanding the Mixed Emotions 68
THE REUNIFICATION PROCESS... 68
   Shift in Active Roles.. 68
   Remain Connected and Supportive 69
THE ALTERNATIVE PATHWAY: ADOPTION.. 70
   Adoption Process 71
PREPARING THE CHILD FOR CHANGE 72
   Reunification Transition.. 72
   Adoption Transition 73

CHAPTER 9: SELF-CARE FOR FOSTER PARENTS: AVOIDING BURNOUT 75

THE IMPORTANCE OF SELF-CARE AND RESILIENCE 76
   Barriers to Good Self-Care 76
RECOGNIZING BURNOUT.. 77
   Compassion Fatigue 79
ACTIVITIES AND RITUALS FOR SELF-CARE.. 79
BUILDING A SUPPORT SYSTEM 81

CHAPTER 10: CONTINUING THE JOURNEY: LIFELONG LEARNING AND ADVOCACY 83

CONTINUOUS TRAINING OPPORTUNITIES AND THEIR IMPORTANCE 84
ADVOCATING FOR FOSTER CHILDREN 85
   Possible Challenging When Advocating... 86
LOOKING BEYOND: BECOMING A MENTOR FOR NEW FOSTER PARENTS 88
   Qualities of a Mentor... 89

CONCLUSION... 91

GLOSSARY 93

REFERENCES 95

IMAGE REFERENCES 95

Introduction

In an ideal world, every child would grow up in a safe, nurturing home where they are cared for, protected, and loved. It's a beautiful dream shared by humanity, where children of all ages have access to resources that help them grow into successful and healthy adults.

However, the reality is that things don't always go as planned, and many children find themselves in situations where they need to be removed from their homes and placed in foster care systems. For some, foster care becomes their only option until they find a forever home through adoption.

If you're considering becoming a foster parent, it's normal to feel overwhelmed by the amount of information available and unsure of where to start. This book is designed to provide you with the necessary skills and knowledge to navigate the complexities of fostering a child, including managing complex relationships and building a strong foundation to support you on your journey as a foster parent.

Chapter 1:

Introduction to Foster Care

Foster care is a complex and emotional experience that involves heart-wrenching stories and courageous individuals. It can be devastating to witness the fear in a child's eyes when they are facing uncertainty and instability. Foster care is about the brave souls who dare tread the waters to ease some of a child's suffering by providing them with the love and stability they're missing. It's about the fear of them curling up in your heart and remaining there forever, making it hard to let them go when the time comes. It's about the constant growth of your heart, with each new face you learn to love—each new story you add to your own.

Considering fostering a child? This chapter aims to clarify what foster care is and debunk common misconceptions.

What Is CPS?

Child Protective Services (commonly known as CPS) is a governmental agency tasked with investigating allegations of child abuse or neglect, intervening where necessary, and providing assistance to parents in the care of their children.

Those who don't understand the role of CPS might regard it as an agency that breaks families apart. However, this is neither their intent nor their goal. CPS's primary focus is always to ensure the well-being and safety of the child. Their first objective is to keep children and parents together, where possible. CPS will work with the families and provide them with resources and services to help the parent rebuild or improve the environment so that the child or children can remain in their care. In certain situations, this is not possible, and it becomes the responsibility of CPS to remove the child from their home and family and place them into foster care for the protection of the child.

How CPS Identifies Children in Need

Unlike law enforcement officers who walk the streets and do regular patrols, CPS relies on reports to guide them toward children in need of their services. They do not get involved unless they've received a tip-off or report that a child is being neglected or abused.

The first step in a CPS investigation is receiving a report. These reports contain five main information points:

- the location of where the suspected neglect took place

- the identity of the child (if available), including age of the child

- the state where it occurred, and where the child is right now (has the incident happened in the same state where the child is currently in)

- who the perpetrator was (needs to be a person that's legally responsible for the child)

- and the allegation being made

Armed with this information, CPS can actively work to identify and locate the child in need and start their investigation. Once they've identified and located the child, they speak to the parents, the child, family members, teachers, neighbors, and any other person who had regular contact with the child to gather as much information as they possibly can.

The outcome of their investigation will determine whether they'll remain in the care of their parents or be removed and enter the foster care system. If there is no evidence of neglect or abuse, the investigation concludes. Suppose there is enough suspicion but nothing concrete. In that case, CPS will maintain regular contact with the child and parents until a definite outcome can be ascertained. However, if the investigation reveals that neglect took place, CPS, determining the severity of the findings, either provides the parents or caregivers training, resources, and services to help them improve the environment and well-being of the child. Or in more severe cases, the child is immediately removed and placed into foster care until a family member is identified who can provide proper care to the child, or the child remains in foster care until reunification can occur. In instances where all measures have been exhausted and reunification could not occur, the parental rights of the parents are terminated, and the child becomes available for adoption.

Why Children Enter Foster Care

There are a myriad of reasons why a child will enter foster care, and understanding these reasons can help you empathize with their experiences and background.

Neglect

One of the most common reasons for a child to enter the foster care system is neglect. Neglect stems from a child lacking adequate food, shelter, supervision, education, or medical care due to the actions or habits of a parent or caregiver. When a child's basic needs are not met, it can lead to impairment or harm.

Abuse

Unfortunately, some children enter the foster care system due to abuse. These traumatic experiences can have lasting psychological effects on a child, impacting the way the child sees themselves and the world around them.

Parental Incapacity

Parents struggling with mental disorders or substance misuse or who are incarcerated can struggle to provide proper care for their children. CPS may need to step in to protect the child from potential harm.

Abandonment or Relinquishment

Some parents or caregivers recognize their inability to care for a child properly and will voluntarily hand them over to foster care. Others, who might not understand the system, will abandon their child in an environment where they believe another will take better care—such as the doorstep of a church, a family member's house, or a local shelter.

Death of Parents

Tragically, some children find themselves in foster care due to the sudden death of both parents, with no immediate family being able to take them in and provide them with the care they need.

Statistics on Foster Care

More than 250,000 enter the United States foster care system every year, of which over 397,000 children are in foster care due to not having permanent families to return to, and only a little over 101,000 of these children are eligible for adoption, according to the National Foster Youth Institution (2023).

According to The Annie E. Casey Foundation, the average time a child spends in foster care is approximately 22 months (2022). While another source puts the average at 15.5 months (Big Fish Local, 2021).

In the last few years, less than 50% of children who leave foster care returned to their parents or previous caregiver, with only one in four children being adopted and one in six leaving foster care to live with a relative or guardian (The Annie E. Casey Foundation, 2022).

With more than 23,000 children that age out of the US foster care system every year, 20% of these children become instantly homeless, and with a one in two chance that they find some form of gainful employment by the age of 24 (National Foster Youth Institution, 2023).

Implications of These Statistics

With such a vast number of children in the foster care system, it puts a strain on the system and resources that are available. With fewer resources than needed, some children aren't placed in foster homes but rather in group homes. Group homes or congregated care places the responsibility of the care of the children in that group on the staff members. While CPS and foster care systems aim to provide each child with a home setting, this is not always the case.

The average duration a child spends in foster care can result in unpredictability and inconsistency, which may adversely affect their mental and psychological health. Conversely, the number of children that age out of foster care indicates a significant percentage of young adults who lack vital life skills and resources to secure employment, deal with mental health problems, and reduce their chances of experiencing homelessness.

The Difference Between Adoption and Foster Care

The lines between adoption and foster care can sometimes blur together, making it difficult to differentiate between the two. However, they serve two very distinct purposes.

Definitions and Long-Term Goals

Foster care refers to a temporary placement of a child's care under a foster parent, who is responsible for providing for and caring for the child. The birth parents of the child still have legal parental rights, but primary care is being provided by the foster parent. The main objective of foster care is to reunite the child with their parents, unless this decision is not in the best interest of the child.

Adoption is a legal and permanent process of placing a child with adoptive parents, where the parental rights are transferred from the birth parents to the adoptive parents. This means that the child becomes a legal member of the adoptive family and is no longer dependent on the child welfare system.

Legal Differences and Permanency

In the foster care system, a child's primary care is temporarily provided by a foster parent. At the same time, the birth parents retain their parental rights, but they must follow a case plan and meet specific criteria within a specified timeframe to reunify with their child. If reunification with the birth parents is not possible, a court of law may terminate their parental rights, and the child becomes eligible for adoption.

When a child is placed in foster care, they are temporarily placed with a family or caregiver while their birth parents work toward reunification. However, in adoption, the legal ties between the child and birth parents are permanently severed, either voluntarily or by court order, and the adoptive parents assume full parental rights and responsibilities. It is also important to note that foster care is a temporary placement, while adoption is a permanent placement.

Misconceptions of Foster Care

Here are a few misconceptions regarding foster care and being a foster parent. When we don't fully understand something, we form beliefs around it that impact the way we see and think about things. Here are the most common misbeliefs:

- **You have to be married.** Your relationship or marital status does not impact your ability to foster a child.

- **Foster children are troubled, damaged, or unfixable.** A child doesn't become a foster child out of their own choices. They find themselves in foster care by no fault of their own.

- **Foster children are delinquents, juveniles, or runaways.** Some foster children have difficult backgrounds that impact how they see and perceive the world around them.

- **You need to be a biological parent in order to be a foster parent.** You do not have to have children of your own in order to become a foster parent.

- **Foster care is expensive.** The state reimburses foster parents in part for the basic necessities of the child, and medical insurance is provided by the state for the child.

- **You need to own a home.** Many foster parents rent instead of owning.

- **You can't have pets.** House pets can be beneficial for foster children, as they can easily find comfort in the unconditional love of a pet, and it provides them with companionship.

- **Foster children can't go on vacations, play sports, get a driver's license, or work part-time.** With permission, foster children can go on vacation, and as for the other activities, foster children are no different from other children.

- **You can't foster if you get too attached.** This is actually a powerful reason to become a foster parent. Take that fear of getting too attached and turn it into fear that a child might never know the unconditional love and care that you can provide them.

- **You can't foster if you've had a challenging life.** With guidance from foster care training, your past challenges can prove to be beneficial as they can assist you in helping and mentoring a foster child through similar struggles.

Embarking the journey of becoming a foster parent is a courageous and demanding undertaking. You will learn just as much from the children you foster as they will learn from you. As you delve deeper into the world of foster care, your comprehension and familiarity with the foster care system will expand. You'll gain a deeper understanding of the complexities of the children in the system. You will discover the essential role you play as a foster parent.

Foster parenting is a journey with challenges and rewards, impacting both the child and parent. In the upcoming chapter, you will gain a better understanding of fostering from the perspective of the child and all that it involves.

Chapter 2:

The Emotional Journey: Understanding the Child's Perspective

Becoming a foster parent requires more than just understanding the system and protocols. It involves empathizing with the child's perspective when they enter foster care, building patience and trust, and comprehending the emotional and mental turmoil that they experience during this transition. By understanding the emotional journey of a foster child, you'll be better equipped to provide them with the care, nurture, and compassion they need to start healing and building healthy attachments to the people and world around them.

Trauma and Its Effects on Children

Most of the children in foster care have already experienced a traumatic event or prolonged traumatic events, whether abuse or neglect, or the tragic death of both parents. A child's removal from their home can be traumatic, especially with minimal notice. It's terrifying for them to be suddenly taken away and moved to a new place, surrounded by strangers.

Experiencing traumatic events can have a long-lasting impact on individuals. Unfortunately, such an impact is greater on children who are still in the process of developing and exploring the world around them. They may not have acquired the necessary life skills to cope effectively with traumatic events or even general life events.

Experiencing trauma can have a significant impact on a child's brain, body, behavior, and thinking. When the trauma is prolonged or continuous, it can disrupt the child's sense of safety, security, and identity, affecting how they perceive and respond to people and situations. Prolonged exposure to trauma can lead to post-traumatic stress disorder (PTSD). PTSD is the term used to describe a disorder in which a person struggles or fails to recover after experiencing or witnessing a traumatic event. Research suggests that between 14-43% of children in the U.S. have experienced trauma, and of those, 3-15% of girls and 1-6% of boys develop PTSD (Hamblen & Barnett, 2023).

Psychological Impacts of Trauma

As a child develops, their brain acts like a sponge that absorbs every experience, emotion, feeling, situation, and thought. These experiences can have either a positive or negative impact on their development. Children who have experienced a traumatic event may exhibit behaviors and thoughts that amplify their reactions to stressful situations. Traumatic stress can lead to persistent sadness, feelings of hopelessness, depression, and physical symptoms, such as flashbacks, nightmares, severe anxiety, or obsessive thoughts.

The Physical Manifestation of Traumatic Stress

Infants depend on their parents or caregivers to understand how they should react or respond to different emotions. When they sense anxiety, anger, or other distressing emotions, they might become fussy, hard to soothe, have disrupted sleeping or eating patterns, or become withdrawn.

Children aged two to five respond the same way in which they are being nurtured and responded to when they are expressing their needs. For example, if their expression of need is met with anger, they start to express their needs with anger. Traumatic stress can cause physical behaviors in this age group.

- irritable outbursts and tantrums
- excessive crying or tearfulness
- heightened sensitivity to loud noises and sounds
- regression to thumb-sucking, baby-talk, or bed-wetting
- increased fear of the dark, being left alone, or monsters
- increased clinginess or separation anxiety
- talking consistently about the event or replaying it

It is possible that children may not comprehend the situation they find themselves in and may expect that things will be resolved (as in they will go home soon), leading them to become distant or even disengaged the longer they remain in this new environment and slowly come to the realization that they won't be going home soon. Traumatic stress may also result in hyperactivity. Children may become excessively active and energetic as a way to cope externally with the intense emotions and thoughts they are experiencing.

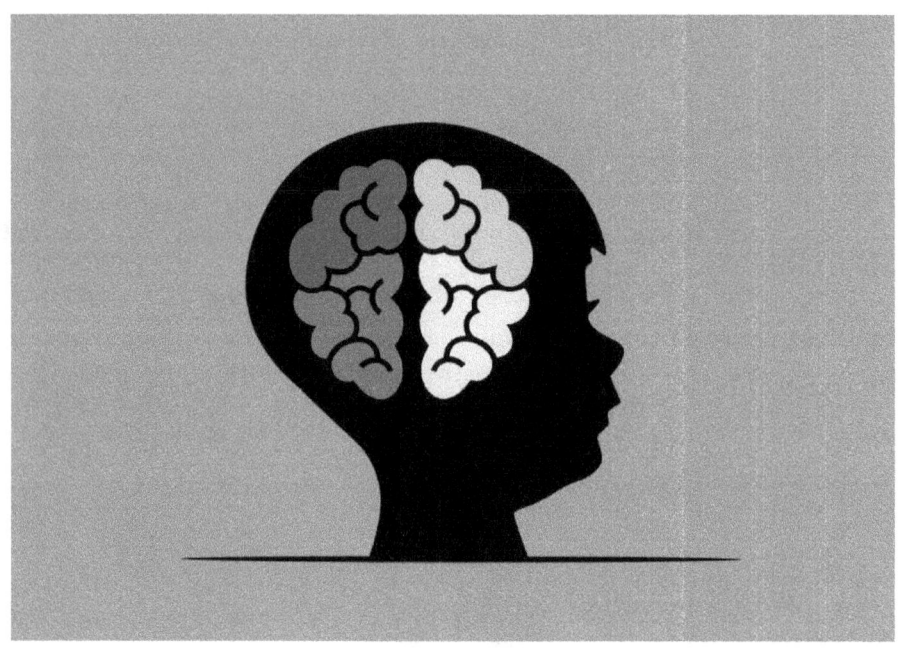

Recognizing Signs of Past Abuse or Neglect

Recognizing the signs of traumatic stress and past abuse or neglect is the initial step toward understanding the kind of care and support a child requires to heal. Understanding is essential for two reasons: firstly, to ensure that the child receives the appropriate care and support, and secondly, to prevent potential triggers that may worsen their trauma.

As a foster parent, you may not have full knowledge of a child's past traumatic experiences. Learning how to identify signs of abuse or neglect is important, as it can help you respond better and potentially prevent triggering situations. However, you're not expected to be an expert. When a child enters care, referrals are submitted right away to assess the child and to provide the child with the necessary services and resources they need to assist with the effects of trauma. As a foster parent, your ability to recognize these signs will help you respond with empathy and compassion. You are not expected to heal or diagnose the child—this should be left to the experts.

Physical Signs

- unexplained bruises, cuts, welts, or injuries, including old scars
- flinching at sudden movements or shying away from touch
- watchful or wary when around others
- hypervigilant, as if waiting for something bad to happen
- wearing inappropriate clothes to cover up their injuries or scars

Emotional Signs

- becoming excessively withdrawn, fearful, or anxious when making a mistake
- displaying excessive behaviors, such as being extremely compliant, demanding, passive, or aggressive
- withdrawing from usual activities or friends
- decrease in their academic performance
- fearful or refusing to be around certain family members
- acting inappropriately, either adult-like or infantile
- engaging in risk-taking behaviors

Recognizing the signs of abuse and neglect is crucial, but it's equally important to understand the long-term effects of trauma on children. Even if a child doesn't exhibit any visible signs of trauma immediately, they may experience its impact later in life, be it years or decades later. They have an increased likelihood of:

- struggling with long-term physical or psychological issues

- struggling with substance abuse issues
- low self-esteem
- fewer healthy coping skills
- struggling with emotional self-regulation
- weak critical thinking skills
- impulsivity
- inability to build healthy attachments and relationships
- low self-motivation
- poor physical health

It is crucial to provide a foster child with a supportive space and environment that can help them recover from the trauma they may have experienced. In addition to this, they should also be given the opportunity to learn and experience how to build secure attachments and rebuild their trust in adults and those around them, especially if it has been broken due to their traumatic experiences.

Attachment and Trust-Building

It is essential to build trust and attachment with your foster child. Trust will enable them to open up and recover from the challenges they're facing. While a secure attachment will enhance the way they form relationships with others, decrease behavioral problems, and improve their mental well-being.

Importance of Secure Attachments

Attachments are emotional bonds with people around us that shape our attachment style. These bonds are formed with caregivers, spouses, children, teachers, friends, etc.

Attachment theory—the study of attachment styles—identified four types of styles: secure, avoidant, ambivalent, and disorganized. Secure is considered a healthy attachment style, while the other three are considered insecure attachment styles.

Foster parents aim to provide secure attachment experiences that help children overcome insecure attachment styles to develop healthy relationships.

An **ambivalent attachment** style is developed in a child when their needs are inconsistently met. Such a child might become particularly fussy or demanding, as they want to make sure that they are not ignored. Additionally, they may exhibit intense emotions and require consistent praise or reassurance that they are doing well.

Avoidant attachment refers to a child who has learned that their needs cannot be met by adults, as their caregiver may have been unresponsive or insensitive to their needs. Such children tend to suppress their emotions or downplay their distress to avoid angering the caregiver. Although they may appear independent and self-sufficient on the surface, this masks their deeper sense of insecurity and distress. A child with avoidant attachment may use a toy or proximity to make contact with their caregiver and stay near them without having to express their needs directly.

Children who experience prolonged emotional distress without receiving adequate support may develop a **disorganized attachment** style. This attachment style is often seen in children who have experienced or witnessed abuse. They view their caregiver as frightening (angry or abusive) or frightened (helpless and unable to provide). Disorganized attachment children display conflicting behaviors, such as fear or distance from their caregiver, but also a desire for control and attention. Some become aggressive toward their caregiver to control the relationship, especially infants who shift from disorganized toward controlling attachment behaviors—where the child attempts to maintain their parent's or caregiver's attention through coercive or hostile behaviors (This attachment shifts back toward disorganized once the infant reaches the age of three to six).

The Importance of Patience and Understanding

It is important to recognize signs of abuse or challenging behavior due to attachment style in children. However, it is equally important to approach the situation with patience and understanding. Direct confrontation or probing may cause the child to distance themselves further and hinder their ability to trust and open up to you. Foster parents should not assume the role of a professional therapist, psychiatrists, or the child's caseworker, and any probing or confrontation should be left to the professionals.

If you are a foster parent, it is important to develop a secure attachment style with the foster child. **Consistency** is the key to building this attachment. You should show up for the child consistently, maintain consistent behavior, and create a safe environment where the child can feel secure physically and emotionally.

Active listening is giving your full attention to the child when they are speaking, whether it's about their day or expressing their feelings. It is important that the child feel heard, validated, and not judged. Encourage them to express themselves freely and avoid making assumptions about their thoughts and emotions. Instead, allow the child to guide you toward understanding their feelings and needs.

It is important to **respect the boundaries** of foster children. These children may have different boundaries than what you are used to, but they have likely established these boundaries in order to feel safe. Therefore, it is important to allow them to set their own boundaries and encourage them to express what they are comfortable with, including physical contact. By respecting their boundaries, you will help the child feel a sense of control, show them that their needs and feelings matter, and build trust.

Be patient with foster children. It takes time and commitment to help them adjust. You might not see the difference you're making right now, but your efforts will eventually pay off.

Keep learning every day. Psychology is constantly evolving, and new techniques are being developed to help children develop healthy attachment styles and recover from trauma. Use available resources to stay informed and to best support the child.

Strategies to Cultivate Trust

Many of the children who are in foster care have experienced betrayal from a caregiver, which has made them hesitant to trust another one. They fear that their trust will be broken again. However, consistency and patience are crucial in developing trust.

It's important to establish a **consistent routine** with foster children, young and old. Children benefit from knowing what to expect and feeling secure about how their days are planned. By creating a routine, you can help ease any uncertainty they may feel and provide a sense of safety and stability in their daily lives.

Create traditions in your children's daily routine, such as bedtime stories, prayers, or game nights. Gradually assign them responsibilities like washing dishes after dinner, but make sure they're ready to avoid overwhelming them.

Displays of **physical affection** can be incredibly powerful to a child and can help them feel loved and cared for. Examples of physical affection include hugs, pats on the back, holding hands, cuddling (if age-appropriate), or forehead kisses. However, it's essential to discuss with the child what they are comfortable with and respect their boundaries to avoid triggering or hindering the development of trust.

It's important to **be transparent** with children about decisions or plans that involve or impact them. Being open with them about what's happening will help them feel included. For instance, if you plan on taking them to the park, discuss it with them beforehand. This will allow them to feel involved and give them a chance to express any concerns or feelings they have.

Fostering a child requires walking in their shoes, understanding their challenges, and providing them with love, trust, and understanding. They may have experienced trauma, but with resilience and support, they can heal.

Chapter 3:

Preparing Your Home and Heart

Becoming a foster parent requires more than just opening your home to a child in need. You'll also have to open your heart. The journey will be fulfilling, but it will also be demanding and require a lot from you and those in your home. You'll need to manage expectations, set boundaries, follow rules, regulations and policies, meet requirements, and follow specific processes. This chapter will guide you through the practical and emotional preparations essential for welcoming a foster child into your home and heart.

Home Study and Safety Requirements

If you're interested in becoming a foster parent and possibly adopting the children you foster, you'll need to meet certain requirements and criteria to become licensed. The biggest step in the process is to undergo a home study.

What Is a Home Study?

A home study, as the name suggests, is a thorough assessment of a potential foster home. This process can take anywhere from two to three months to complete and involves various components to help the verifying agency determine if the environment is safe and suitable for a foster child. Additionally, these home studies assist the caseworkers and the placement unit in identifying a foster child who will be a good match for the family.

Specialists perform home studies to collect information about you, your home, your household members, and your community. This information is used to create a report that will determine whether you and your home are suitable for fostering. The report may also include suggestions for improvements or reasons why the verification agency said no to your application.

Key Areas of Assessment

A home study consists of the following:
- training and interviews
- a home visit
- background checks
- medical reports

- financial statements

- references

Training and Interviews

Many agencies offer orientation sessions for individuals interested in becoming foster parents. These sessions provide a comprehensive understanding of the agency, the fostering process, and what to expect during the verification process. Attending these sessions is a great way to learn more about fostering, receive answers to common questions, and gain an estimate of how long the process will take.

Foster parent applicants typically need to attend training sessions that cover topics such as CPR, first-aid, parenting, cultural and racial awareness, and special needs care.

During the fostering process, interviews will be conducted with you, your spouse or partner, and any children or family members who live in the home where the fostering will take place. These interviews will give the specialist conducting the home study an understanding of who you are, your motivations, and the type of home environment you can provide.

A Home Visit

During a home visit, a specialist will come to your home to check whether certain safety and security precautions are in place. They will have a checklist with them to mark off the items that meet the safety standards. The specialist may also take pictures of the inside and outside the home to keep in the report.

If you plan to foster a child, then your home should meet all the state licensing standards, be free from hazards, offer a child-friendly environment appropriate for the age range of the child you wish to foster, and meet health and fire safety regulations. Some states and agencies may require an inspection to be performed by the local health and fire departments in addition to the home visit by the specialist.

While not always feasible, it is widely believed that providing a separate space for a foster child to call their own can better help the child adapt to the new environment. Having their own space gives them the freedom to express themselves, a place that is exclusively theirs, and a sanctuary where they can feel secure during their transition period.

The specialist is not there to judge your housekeeping. They are only concerned with the safety, comfort, and child-friendliness of your living space.

Background Checks

Background checks are required for you, your partner, and anyone else living in the home who's 14 or older. Criminal and child abuse records will be checked at all government levels, and fingerprints are required.

Medical Reports and Financial Statements

You'll be required to submit a medical statement from a doctor stating that you are in good health and have a normal life expectancy. If you have a chronic condition that's under control, it's unlikely to concern the specialist. If you or anyone in the home has sought out help for mental health issues, a specialist might want records of visits to a professional—this is often viewed as a strength to seek out help.

You'll also be asked to provide financial statements as a means of showing that you're financially stable (able to pay bills, cover the costs of an additional child, and maintain regular repayments), along with proof of insurance for home, life, auto, and health.

References

References are either letters or interviews that are conducted with people who aren't related to you, but who will provide valuable insight into who you are as a person and possible caregivers. These references will assist the specialist in forming a clear image of who you are, the type of environment you provide, and your readiness to take on the additional responsibilities.

A bad reference alone won't disqualify someone from becoming a foster parent. It's considered along with other information to determine its relevance to the home study report.

Preparing for the Home Study

When you're undergoing a home study, the agency you're working with may provide you with a checklist of documentation and regulations that you need to have in place. If you're not given a checklist, you can search for one online. It's crucial that you ensure that all the required items are in place for the home study. These lists can be extensive, particularly when it comes to child safety, but it's critical to maintain a high level of safety in the home at all times.

Openness and Feedback

It's important to be honest when discussing difficult topics with the home study specialist, such as marriage, parenting styles, and your motivations for fostering. The specialist is not trying to find flaws in your character but rather how you handle challenges, if you have a support system, if you can recognize when you need help, and how you will ensure the child's safety and protection. Remember, we are all human and make mistakes. Honesty is crucial, and it will help create a better environment for the child.

The home study report is an assessment of your readiness and may contain recommendations. Review these recommendations as areas for improvement, not criticism. Its goal is to make you aware of any necessary improvements in terms of safety standards being met before you can foster a child.

Becoming a foster parent is a process, and setbacks may arise. However, as long as you keep pushing forward and remain determined, you will find that it is all worth it when you see a foster child in need grow to become strong, healthy, and happy.

Adjusting Your Family Dynamics

When you decide to open your home to a foster child, the dynamics of your family will change. It is important to have conversations with your own children and spouse (if applicable), help them through this transition, reassure them, and allow them to set boundaries that will help them welcome the foster child into the family. You will need to establish clear expectations, prioritize family time, and set boundaries with the foster child entering your home.

Involving Your Own Children

Many parents who choose to foster a child have concerns about how it might affect their own children. One of the main concerns is that the foster child might have a negative influence on their own children.

However, from the experience and testimonies of other foster parents, it's often quite the opposite. In fact, your own children can be a positive influence on the foster child. They often develop a caring relationship with the foster child, treating them like a sibling. They'll dedicate their time and patience to the foster child and guide them in doing what's right.

Adding a foster sibling to your family is fantastic, but your children may have concerns, worries, and fears about the impact on them and their relationship with you.

Open Conversations

It is important to have an open conversation with your children when you decide to bring a foster child into your home. Provide them with all the necessary details so that they can fully understand what this means. The most crucial part of this conversation, however, is to listen to their thoughts and feelings about the situation.

It is important to listen to your children's concerns and questions about your decision to foster a child. Validate their feelings and reassure them. Keep in mind that your desire to foster a child may make your child feel uneasy sharing their feelings. They may struggle with feelings of guilt, not wanting to share you, their room, or toys with another child. As a parent, it is your responsibility to provide reassurance and validation to your child, listen to their concerns, and not force them to accept a foster sibling if they are not ready.

Even though words are powerful, sometimes they aren't enough to make your children feel secure. Reassure them that they will continue to receive your love and attention the same way after a new child enters your home. It is important to repeatedly reassure your children that your love for them will remain the same and that you will not love them any less or give them less attention because of a foster child joining your family.

Establish Boundaries

Take time after a meal to sit down and discuss with your children what they are willing to and not willing to tolerate when it comes to bringing a foster child into the home. Respect your child's needs and preferences, such as if they don't want to share their toys or have someone in their room. By setting boundaries, your child will feel safe and heard, and you'll have a better understanding of how to approach the introduction of a foster child into your family.

Preparing for Change

Introducing a foster child into your home requires you to establish clear boundaries and expectations. It's important to keep in mind that foster children have experienced trauma, which can make it difficult for them to adjust to their new environment. Since trauma affects each child differently, what might have worked for one child may not work for another.

Set Clear Expectations

It's important to have a conversation with your foster child about their personal boundaries. Ask them what they are comfortable with and what they are not. Take note of their limits and willingness to take on responsibilities or help out around the house. It's also important to explain the morning and bedtime routines, including what time they should go to bed and wake up. If they're ready, ask if they would like to help with chores and what they're willing to do. However, it's important not to expect too much of them from the onset. Give them time to adjust to their new environment and grow comfortable before placing additional expectations on them.

Prioritize Family Time

It's essential to organize activities and traditions that promote bonding between you and the foster child, as well as between the foster child and your own children. Intentional interactions and open communication should be encouraged to build trust and help them adjust to their new environment. This will facilitate bonding and ensure a positive experience for everyone involved.

Financial and Legal Preparations

If you're considering foster care, it's important to understand that it's not about making money. Financial incentives, such as compensation, reimbursements, or subsidies, should not be your main motivation. The state provides a monthly stipend based on the child's age and basic needs, but it may not cover all their expenses. When caring for a special needs foster child, specialized compensation is available to help with therapies, medical visits, and other specific needs. Additionally, the foster child's healthcare is covered by the state since they are legally considered to be a child of the state.

Legal Protections and Rights

As a foster parent, you have certain rights. If needed, you can reach out to the agency or specialist for more information regarding your rights.

1. **Right to no coercion, discrimination, or reprisal.** You have a right to submit complaints to the Office of Family and Children Ombudsman.

2. **Right to confidentiality.** Home studies gather very personal information about you and your household members. You have the right to have your personal information kept confidential (to the extent of the law).

3. **Right to be informed.** You have the right to be informed about any health concerns a foster child poses to themselves or others before they are placed within your care.

4. **Right to training and support.** You have the right to receive the right training and be equipped with the necessary skills to support a foster child who has an emotional, mental, or physical handicap.

5. **Right to decline placement.** You have the right to decline the placement of a foster child if you believe that the foster child will not be a good fit. This right also includes declining to keep a child in your care if the situation is no longer conducive for both of you.

Emotional Readiness

Take a moment to think about why you want to become a foster parent. If you're considering fostering as a way of replacing a recent loss, it's important to seek counseling first. Make sure your motivations are genuine and that you're emotionally prepared for the challenges you'll face. This will give both you and the specialist peace of mind.

It's important to keep in mind that foster care is a temporary arrangement. The ultimate goal is to reunite the foster child with their birth parents. As a foster parent, you may find yourself welcoming new children into your home several times a year. Fostering is not a one-time event, but rather a continuous process of opening your home and heart to children in need, reuniting them with their birth parents, and then starting the process anew.

When you become a foster parent, it's natural to develop an attachment to the child you are caring for. However, it's important to maintain privacy and respect boundaries between you and the child. Setting clear behavioral expectations can help both you and the child understand what is expected of them. To avoid heartbreak when the child is eventually reunited with their biological parents, it's crucial to maintain emotional boundaries. While attachment is normal, it should never interfere with the child's journey toward being reunited with their parents.

Preparing your home and family for fostering is a complex journey that requires adjustments, patience, and a deep understanding of your role and responsibilities. As you go through this process, it's important to remember that at the heart of fostering lies the need to provide love, care, and a better future for a child in need.

Chapter 4:

The First Days: Building a Safe Haven

Welcoming a foster child into your home is the start of a profound journey filled with twists and turns but also magical and heartwarming moments. The first few days to months that a child spends in your home are critical. During this time, you need to lay the foundation for a lasting, loving, and positive impact. This chapter will delve into the nuances of the early days, with an emphasis on making the child feel welcome, building bonds, dealing with initial behavioral challenges, and ways in which you can soothe their anxieties.

Welcoming a Child to Your Home

When a foster child is brought to your home by their social worker, they have likely had a difficult and tiring day. They may be feeling scared, anxious, and overwhelmed as they are about to stay with strangers for a short period. Even if they have been in the foster care system for some time, you and your family are still strangers to them. Therefore, it is important to make them feel welcome and comfortable during your first meeting. You should aim to create a safe and friendly environment that allows them to be themselves. This initial meeting is crucial in establishing a positive relationship.

Welcoming Ideas

Welcome Book

If you are notified about a child entering your home, and you have a few days to prepare, you may have more information about the child than they'll have about you. In such a situation, it's a good idea to create a welcome book for them. This book should contain photos with short descriptions of everyone in the household, including pets, and details of things the child might like about where they'll be living and going to school.

A welcome book can help the foster child get to know you before they meet you in person. This can reduce their anxieties as they'll have a better idea of what to expect when they arrive at your doorstep.

Welcome Box

A welcome box is an excellent way to greet a child who's coming into your home. If you know any personal information about the child, like their preferences or favorite colors, you can customize the box accordingly. Alternatively, you can include the essential toiletries they'll need along with a couple of comforting items like a toy, blanket, or plushy. You may also want to add a few things to help them personalize their room if they wish to do so. Make sure to reassure them that everything in the box belongs to them and won't be taken away.

Home Tour and Safety Overview

Provide the foster child with a tour of the house. Show them the different rooms of the house and the room they'll be sleeping in. Show them the bathroom and where they might find essential items that they may need, as well as how to use the shower and which taps have hot and cold water. Show them common areas where they'll be free to watch TV, do crafts, or simply play. Be mindful of showing them where emergency items are, such as a fire extinguisher or what to do in an emergency.

Don't overwhelm them, but provide them with an overview of these things, and as you show them each area of the house and explain the major rules around them, allow the child an opportunity to ask any questions if they have them.

One way to make a child feel welcome is by showing them around the kitchen and letting them know where they can find snacks and food. It's a good idea to stock up on some of their favorite food items, too. You can make them feel even more welcome by putting a picture of them on the fridge alongside other family pictures. After the home tour is done, give them the space to unpack their things. If they allow you, you can help them. Otherwise, just let them settle in on their own.

Setting Boundaries, Routines, and Expectations

On the first day of a child's arrival, it's important to establish the house rules, boundaries, expectations, and routines. This will help prevent any unintentional overstepping of rules or boundaries by the child. Clearly communicate what the rules and expectations are. For instance, if you expect the child to help you with some chores, make it clear to them. However, keep in mind that they are still adjusting and may not be able to handle additional stress.

It's important to have a conversation with the child to understand their expectations and boundaries. If they are older, let them explain their routine and try to respect their boundaries. Find common ground with expectations and set a routine that they will need to follow. For younger children, a visual representation of their daily schedule might help. Make sure to be clear about meals and bedtimes. It's best to start using the bedtime routine on the first night, even if they struggle to sleep. Having a routine in place can help them feel safe and find predictability.

Building Bonds

During the first few days and weeks of fostering a child, it is important to create opportunities for bonding experiences as much as possible. It is essential to have some alone time with the child so that you can listen to their concerns or fears. Additionally, it is crucial to provide them with an opportunity to bond with your partner, other family members, and children in the house.

Introduce pets slowly to children. Ensure the child is comfortable with them to prevent any trauma. A dog's excited behavior may confuse a child unfamiliar with pets.

It's important to take the time to discover what activities and hobbies a foster child likes, as well as any new activities they might be interested in trying out. This will give you opportunities to bond with them. Some examples of activities you could do together include mini golf, having a picnic in the park, going bowling, visiting a play park, watching their favorite movie or TV show with them, or having a game night.

Understanding and Managing Initial Behaviors

Do you know the feeling of excitement when a rollercoaster goes up, and your stomach flips nervously when it rushes down? Well, the first few days and even months with a new foster child can be similar to that. There'll be moments when you'll be amazed at how easily they seem to find their groove within your home, but you'll also face moments when they display challenging behaviors that can feel overwhelming.

Early Behavioral Challenges

The first night will be the hardest. They'll struggle to fall asleep and feel overwhelmed being in a strange and unfamiliar place. They might throw tantrums or be disruptive as they try to fight falling asleep. This is all normal. Stress and fear manifest in different ways.

During the first few days or weeks of fostering a child, everything may seem calm and easy. This is often referred to as the honeymoon period, during which the child may be reserved and shy in their new surroundings. They may behave well and get along with your own children. However, as time passes, and they become more comfortable and secure in their new environment, their true personality will start to emerge. This may also bring learned behaviors that are not always positive. You may experience tantrums, crying, fighting, depression, anxiety, and a range of other emotions.

These behaviors are often a result of feeling overwhelmed, fearful, stressed, or uncertain. Sometimes, they stem from a child's past experiences where they had to display such behaviors to get their needs met or gain attention from their caregivers. Other times, children may test boundaries and rules to see what they can get away with, or they may show highly independent behaviors because they've learned to care for themselves. The best way to manage these types of behaviors is by being consistent in routines and boundaries.

Routines can be very beneficial for foster children, as well as any child. By providing a predictable schedule, you can create a sense of security for the child. When they learn that they can rely on you as a caregiver and the routine you establish, they are more likely to respect boundaries and behave appropriately. This can help reduce disruptive behavior and create a more stable environment for the child.

Strategies for Behavioral Challenges

Use available resources such as agencies, counselors, social workers, and professionals to manage challenging behaviors. Maintain routine, set boundaries, and try other strategies to understand and manage behaviors effectively.

Manifestations of Their Trauma

In Chapter 2, we discussed how trauma affects people differently. Behaviors that you see in others may stem from their past trauma. As a foster parent, show empathy and kindness instead of punishment. Enforce rules and boundaries in a way that does not cause harm but shows that you care for their safety and well-being.

Praise and Positive Reinforcement

As a foster parent, you will often need to say "no" to your foster child, for example, "No, don't do that," "No, you can't have that now," or "No, that was not nice." However, it is important to also focus on providing positive reinforcement. When you say "no," try to find ways to offer them alternatives. For many foster children, positive reinforcement is something they have rarely experienced. They may have never been told that someone is proud of them, that they are doing a good job, or even just a simple "thank you."

Encouraging positive behaviors with praise can help children understand which actions are disruptive and which are desirable.

Active Listening

Having a conversation with them can be very helpful. You may be overthinking their behavior, or they may not have a clear understanding of the situation. A simple, meaningful conversation can make a big difference. It is important to be aware of the boundaries they have set for themselves and how they may have been crossed, leading to their current behavior. It may take some time and a lot of patience to establish effective communication, but it will make things easier for both of you in the long run.

Understand and Observe

If they are withdrawn or refuse to communicate with you, it may be due to feelings of guilt, fear, or shame that are preventing them from expressing their needs. In such situations, it is important to observe and understand their non-verbal cues, such as body language, facial expressions, and other behaviors. For instance, pay attention to whether they flinch at sudden movements or loud noises, whether they maintain a guarded posture, whether they suddenly grow pale or shake during certain situations, or whether their facial expression contradicts their words. By being attentive to these cues, you can better understand and support the person.

It's important to keep in mind that many foster children may not have ever had healthy boundaries or know how to establish them. Being observant enough to catch their non-verbal cues indicating they are in distress can help both you and the child establish boundaries that make them feel more comfortable. This can also help you gain insight into the possible trauma they have experienced, which can help you better empathize, support, and care for them.

The early days of fostering are chaotic but crucial. It requires patience, consistency, empathy, compassion, and structure. Every small breakthrough with the child will outweigh the struggles.

Chapter 5:

Navigating Relationships: Birth Families and Caseworkers

The primary goal of fostering is to reunite the child with their birth families. To achieve this goal, it is essential to maintain, strengthen, and foster various relationships throughout the journey. This chapter focuses on the importance of maintaining relationships between foster children and their birth families, as well as developing a healthy relationship between you and the caseworker.

The Importance of Maintaining Birth Family Connections

Fostering a child requires a collective effort. As a foster parent, you establish a rapport with the foster child while simultaneously assisting them in maintaining and enhancing their connections with their biological family. An option as well is for you to develop a relationship with the birth family; however, depending on the circumstances and on a case to case basis, you might not have any direct contact with the birth family.

The Role of Birth Families in a Child's Life

We rely on family members for information to form our identity. As we grow, tidbits received from others help shape who we are—now, consider the emotional impact on foster children when they are separated from their birth families. These children often experience a sense of loss of their identity and struggle to understand where they come from and who they are. This can have a significant impact on their emotional and mental well-being, making it crucial for them to receive proper care and support during this difficult time.

Foster children need to maintain connections with their birth families as it can help them develop self-esteem by reducing feelings of loss, rejection, self-blame, and abandonment. Therefore, whenever possible, the relationships between a foster child and their birth family should be preserved, improved, and strengthened. By facilitating these relationships, you can provide your foster child with a greater sense of stability and belonging, even though they have been removed from their original home and placed in your care.

Navigating the Challenges

Maintaining relationships with birth families can be challenging, and sometimes, communication with them can bring up negative emotions.

It is common for birth parents to struggle at times, and this can have an impact on the foster child. As a supportive foster parent, your role during contact sessions with the birth parents is crucial. Your attitude and views toward the birth parents will affect your relationship with the child, and how the child views their birth parents. In order to provide the necessary support that the foster child needs, it is important to speak positively about their birth families.

Attitude Matters

It is important to always speak positively about a foster child's birth family and highlight their strengths. In cases where you cannot highlight strengths, it's important that you lean on the phrase *if you don't have anything nice to say, don't say anything*. Avoid speaking negatively about them to create a safe space where the foster child feels comfortable discussing their birth family with you. When you have a positive attitude toward the birth family, the foster child is more likely to maintain a connection with them. Additionally, empathize with the birth family and understand how they might be feeling, while being sensitive to all sides. Making them feel welcome is essential.

Teaching Moments

As you build relationships with the birth family, you will know you have made progress when they seek your help in creating a safer and more loving home for their children or seek advice on raising their children in a more loving manner. These moments indicate that reunification may eventually be possible.

Importance of Siblings

Keeping siblings together is one of the essential goals in foster care, but sometimes, it's not possible due to various reasons. However, it's crucial to ensure that siblings stay connected and have a constant relationship with each other. You can collaborate with the other foster family to facilitate regular interaction for the siblings, if the foster child in your care has been separated from their sibling, so that their bond is maintained, along with that of the birth parents. In most cases, siblings have known each other their entire lives, and having that connection severed can be a traumatic experience. Encouraging regular time together, even over video chats, can significantly help both siblings find stability and a sense of self in their circumstances. Siblings going through the same transition can provide a deeper sense of comfort for each other because they both experienced the same circumstances and are learning to adapt.

Tips for Bonding Moments

- Where access plans are in place, encourage phone calls, video chats, and letters between the child and their birth family.

- Where possible, drive the child to and from their visitations so you can be there to provide support before and after.

- Get in touch with the birth family and offer to share updates with them, whether these are sharing pictures or inviting them to join in on school or extracurricular activities. This may require approval, so check before arranging these.

- Encourage the birth family to be present for court hearings. Just showing up can mean a lot to the child.

The Role of the Caseworker in Your Foster Journey

The role of a caseworker or foster care social worker in your foster care journey is to act as a liaison between you, the social service agencies, birth families, and, in certain cases, adoption families. The caseworker may also be involved in situations where social service agencies conduct investigations on reports of child abuse or neglect or when a child needs to be removed from their home due to safety reasons.

Understanding the Caseworker's Responsibilities

As with home studies, the caseworker will routinely check in on the foster child to ensure that they are settling in and that their needs are being met. They may also note whether the child needs special attention, or if they're struggling mentally and emotionally to transition into foster care.

The caseworker's interactions with the foster child are crucial in determining the child's developing needs and assessing their progress in school, behavior, and emotional state. The caseworker will have conversations with the foster child to address any concerns they may have regarding their situation and reunification prospects.

A caseworker has three main areas of focus when working with foster care situations: the child, the foster parents, and the birth family. Their primary goal is to ensure that the child's safety and needs are being met. They provide assistance and guidance to foster parents and ensure they receive adequate training and skill-building sessions so they can provide the best care for the children in their care. Additionally, the caseworker is responsible for working with the birth family to create a reunification plan that includes support groups, treatments, and services that the birth parents will need to attend to meet certain reunification goals, allowing their children to return to their care.

The primary goal of a caseworker is to establish an atmosphere that facilitates the reunion of children and their parents. This objective involves several aspects, such as identifying suitable foster parents to take care of the child and encouraging the birth parents to enhance their lives and circumstances so that they can create a secure and supportive environment for their child. Moreover, the caseworker must maintain healthy relationships between the child, foster parents, and birth families while ensuring that all policies, regulations, and state laws of social service agencies are being followed and met.

Build a Collaborative Relationship

Caseworkers have immense responsibilities and represent several foster children. To maintain a healthy relationship, both parties have to rely on each other and provide adequate information for the right decision to be made.

If you are feeling overwhelmed, concerned, or need guidance, do not hesitate to reach out to your caseworker for help. Preventing a child from bouncing around from one foster home to another is a priority for the caseworker, and that includes ensuring that you have the support and skills to continue providing care. Even if you and the caseworker don't see eye to eye, it's important to maintain a collaborative relationship and work together toward a shared goal. This will ease the caseworker's mind, yours, and the foster child's when everyone is able to work together without animosity.

Navigating Disagreements and Conflicts

It is natural to have disagreements and conflicts with the caseworker, CASA, or even the guardian ad litem when you are involved in foster care. However, it is important to view these disagreements as opportunities for personal growth and gaining knowledge. During a disagreement or conflict, you should aim to redirect the conversation toward a more constructive and positive direction. You can achieve this by following five simple steps.

- **Take a break.** Disagreements and conflicts often arise when emotions run high, and perspective is lost. Creating distance can help regulate emotions and find perspective.

- **Become aware of your emotions.** Reflect on your emotions and identify the underlying feelings. Look deeper: Is there any hurt, disregard, or feeling of being undervalued?

- **Listen to what's being said and not said.** It is important to actively listen to what the other person is communicating to you. Be mindful of your own emotions, but do not let them prevent you from truly hearing what is being said. Avoid making assumptions or jumping to conclusions while the other person is talking. Seek to understand their perspective and emotions, and try to comprehend their reactions as well.

- **Find common ground.** Remember, you both want the same thing: a healthy, loved, and supported child. Refocus on these shared values and work through disagreements together, knowing that you're on the same side.

- **Constructive feedback.** Be open to constructive feedback. Focus on specific behaviors and actions that can be improved upon to prevent future disagreements.

Relationships can be complex, especially when it comes to building a relationship with a child in your care. It may be challenging at first, but it's crucial that you establish collaborative relationships between you and the caseworker. Additionally, it's important to encourage the child to maintain their relationship with their birth family. Building any relationship requires effort, attention, and patience, and there may be some obstacles along the way, but these challenges should not detract from the shared goal that each of you has.

Chapter 6:

Educational and Developmental Gap Challenges

Each foster child is a book of unique experiences, memories, and moments, and these shape their educational and developmental needs. As a foster parent, you play an active role in the foster child's educational journey. This chapter provides an in-depth look at how to support and champion a foster child's learning and development.

Addressing Educational Gaps

Children in foster care often face stigma and discrimination in school despite the efforts of child welfare agencies, foster parents, and other support systems. In many cases, these children have experienced a lack of education prior to entering the foster care system. This may include missed school days or a lack of access to educational resources. Additionally, some children may have special educational needs (SEN) that have not yet been identified. It is essential that any education gaps or SEN are identified as early as possible so that the child can receive the appropriate support and services to succeed in school.

Legal Rights and Involvements

It can be challenging to manage a foster child's education when their birth parents maintain rights over them. As a foster parent, you don't have the same rights as the birth parents, which can make it difficult to determine whether the child is performing well in school or if any learning or thinking differences have been identified.

Things you may have a legal right to is as a foster parent:

- signing educational forms
- consenting to evaluations and services
- being able to request an evaluation to be performed
- attending evaluation or individualized educational planning (IEP) team meetings

Whenever possible, it's important to work with the caseworker to gain permission to access the child's school records, be informed of any special educational needs that were identified, and attend school meetings. The CPS is given temporary managing conservatorship (TMC) rights over the foster child. The birth parents will be updated on their child during the permanency hearings. While you may not have certain legal rights, you can engage with the teachers and the child to find out how they are doing in school, whether they are receiving the necessary support, and explore ways in which you can provide additional support at home.

Recognizing the Signs

It's important to be mindful of the indicators that suggest a learning gap in a foster child's education. There are three types of signs you should watch out for when assessing whether the gap in their learning is due to disruptions in their schooling, or if it could be caused by undiagnosed learning or thinking disabilities.

The first thing to pay attention to is the **academic performance** of the child. It is important to keep track of their grades and marks for different assessments such as assignments, quizzes, and tests. However, it is essential to not solely rely on grades, as they can be misleading and may not represent the actual educational gap that exists. Instead, compare their academic performance with age-appropriate tasks to identify any gaps in their education. This will give you a better understanding of the areas they need to improve on.

Secondly, look for **behavioral cues** in which the child may frequently complain about stomachaches or headaches to avoid going to school, or they might say they're "too dumb to do this" or that they "can't do that." These can be indicators that there is a gap in their education, which is adding additional strain on their performance and well-being, and they might not know how to articulate that they require help. Showing aggression or dislike toward homework or simple school tasks may also be indicative of either a gap in their education or a learning or thinking disability that is making them hyper-aware that they aren't on the same level as those around them.

Lastly, pay attention to the **feedback** you receive from educators. Stay in regular communication with their teachers to stay in the know of what the child's educational needs are and whether further action is required to support and help the child bridge this gap.

Children who are in foster care often have special educational needs due to various reasons, such as trauma, neglect, hereditary conditions, missed education, and undiagnosed or untreated diagnoses. It is important to recognize and identify these needs early on so that the foster care agency and you can take the necessary steps to help the child bridge the gap and receive the support they require.

Strategies to Bridge the Gaps

It is important to be knowledgeable and able to assist in bridging the gap. Three strategies exist to assess the gap.

- **Assessment.** In most cases, you will need to obtain permission from the child's caseworker who has TMC to conduct this assessment. The purpose of this assessment is to identify the specific areas within the child's education that may require additional attention and could potentially be a concern for both teachers and parents. Addressing these areas can help prevent further difficulties for the child as they progress to the next grade.

- **Tutoring.** Tutoring can be an essential tool for any child who needs to catch up and improve their academic performance. There are professional and personal tutors available, as well as peer tutoring. Peer tutoring can be particularly helpful for foster children who have been transferred to a new school. Classmates who have good grades and are capable of helping them catch up on missed work can provide them with class notes. Some teachers may also offer tutoring sessions.

- **Personalized learning.** If a foster child has been diagnosed with learning or thinking disabilities, it is essential to understand that general study routines may not be effective for them. Each difficulty requires a unique approach. For instance, a child with attention difficulties may not be able to remain focused for long hours, and a child who is a visual thinker may not benefit from pages and pages of written content.

Supporting Special Education Needs

A learning disability in a child occurs when they struggle more than their peers or have a disability that prevents them from benefiting from mainstream education. Disabilities can be physical or mental impairments, such as difficulties with mobility, conversation, or sensory processing, as well as learning disorders like ADHD, speech issues, autism, and dyslexia.

Early identification and support for educational challenges is crucial. It helps children prepare themselves and receive the necessary guidance and help. Without proper support, the gap may widen, leading to further struggles. Timely support is crucial for a child's academic success.

Strategies for Support

To create a nurturing environment for foster children, it's important to prioritize their educational plan, their engagement with specialists and therapists, and a home environment that caters to their needs.

An **Individualized Educational Plan (IEP)** is a program that offers free assistance to students who require extra help and support in school due to special needs. This program is provided to families with children in public schools and contains a list of goals and support services that may be required to ensure the child's success in school. The IEP plan provides educators and parents with effective strategies and services that can help in the child's educational development.

Specialists or therapists can offer lessons, strategies, and therapy sessions to help children overcome their difficulties or find the best ways to live and cope with their disabilities. Both you and the child can benefit from the valuable insights and information provided by a speech therapist or occupational therapist.

Home Environment

Caring for a child with special educational needs or other special needs can be a challenging task. However, creating a home environment that meets these needs is essential to ensure the child's comfort and well-being. Having a basic understanding of how to create a conducive home environment can make a big difference in how the child approaches their day-to-day life and overcomes the challenges they face.

Some strategies you can incorporate are:

- **Modify toys and equipment.** For better control of fine motor skills, start with bigger blocks and gradually reduce the size. Covering a sippy cup or bottle with a sock can help your child hold it with ease.

- **Visual choice boards.** To help children who have speech impairment or behavioral challenges, it is recommended to create visual choice boards for activities, toys, clothes, and foods. By using these boards, children can communicate their needs without being verbal, which can reduce their frustration. Additionally, seeing their choices can make it easier for them to make a decision, compared to feeling overwhelmed. Ensure balanced food choices by controlling available options.

- **Visual schedules.** Children often feel safe and comfortable when they have a routine that they can predict. This helps them avoid uncertainty and confusion about what will happen next. A visual schedule can also help young children have a clear idea of what activities they should expect and where they will take place. You can place a visual schedule on the wall of your child's room, the kitchen, or play area to help them stay on track.

- **Transition cues.** Some children may find it challenging to deal with interruptions or changes in their routine. The most effective way to help them understand and cope with these changes is by giving them advance notice that their current activity or stimulation will be ending soon. You can let them know, for example, that they have five minutes left before lunchtime or before they need to start a new activity. Then, when one minute remains, you can let them know and start preparing them for the transition. This gradual approach helps them prepare for the change and reduces anxiety or stress associated with sudden changes.

- **Chill corner.** Create a private chill space in your home for your child to calm down when overwhelmed. Add a comfort item or encourage reading in this area.

The Importance of Life Skills

It's not uncommon for foster children to have gaps in their education and life skills. One way to help them overcome these gaps is by involving them in daily chores around the house, such as cooking, cleaning, and organizing. By doing so, they can acquire important life skills, such as budgeting, laundry, communication, and problem-solving. These skills can increase their confidence and independence and help them feel more capable and self-assured. As they learn and master new skills, they'll become more confident in their ability to learn and grow.

Learning a new life skill and gaining independence can give a child a boost in confidence. This newfound confidence and empowerment can help them in other areas of their lives. For instance, a foster child who previously didn't know how to do their own laundry can feel empowered after successfully accomplishing this task. This feeling of accomplishment can motivate them to try harder in other areas they are struggling with, such as a difficult math problem or assignment.

A few core life skills that can be invaluable for a foster child are:

- cooking
- cleaning
- money management
- time management
- problem-solving and decision-making
- social and communication skills
- self-care and well-being
- transportation and navigation
- career development and personal goals

Consider the life skills you acquired while growing up, and reflect on the skills you wish you had learned earlier in life. Then, find ways to teach these valuable life skills to your foster child in order to increase their independence, confidence, and motivation to learn and grow.

A child's education and development involve many different aspects. As foster parents, it is important to be actively involved, to understand the unique needs of the child, and to work together with educational institutions and services. Providing these efforts can make a significant difference in the child's educational future. Every child deserves a chance for a brighter educational future, regardless of their past or the challenges they have faced.

Chapter 7:

Celebrating Milestones and Creating Memories

Foster children have experienced a lot of disruptions in their lives. In addition to the traumatic experiences they've endured, they've also lost smaller things like family traditions, rituals that bring them comfort, and their sense of self. As a foster parent, your role is to identify and encourage the child's interests and talents, celebrate their milestones and small wins, and create lasting bonds and memories with them.

Recognizing Small Wins

When a child is placed in foster care, their world is often turned upside down. This can lead to a lack of confidence, struggles with their sense of self, and an inability to recognize or realize their talents due to a lack of nurturing. Encouragement is key to enhancing a child's confidence, motivation, determination, sense of self, and resilience. Children need to feel that what they do matters and that they are capable of doing great things.

The Power of Positive Reinforcement

Positive reinforcement is a great way to boost a child's confidence, motivate them to perform better, show that you care, and minimize negative behaviors. This technique involves rewarding good or desired behavior. By using positive reinforcement with your foster child, you can help them develop social and emotional skills, learn what is expected of them, and learn how to interact positively with others.

There are three ways to utilize positive reinforcement while dealing with children:

- **Praising** the child when they exhibit good behavior. This can be expressed through verbal appreciation, such as telling them that they did well or that you are proud of them, or non-verbal appreciation, such as a high-five, a pat on the back, or a hug.

- Providing **rewards** for positive behavior can encourage children to work toward displaying positive behaviors. You can use a sticker chart to reward them with a sticker for positive behaviors such as tidying up their toys, getting dressed, saying thank you, and so forth.

- For older foster children, positive behavior can result in **privileges**. For example, their positive behavior could earn them more screen or video game time and the chance to stay up later on weekends or attend a school event or concert.

When you use positive reinforcement as a behavior modification technique, it's important to be consistent in how you apply it and in the specific behaviors you reward. Inconsistency in positive reinforcement can have negative consequences that might result in the aggravation of the very behaviors you're trying to eliminate.

Celebrating Growth and Resilience

It is a common misconception that a child who has gone through a traumatic experience is automatically resilient. However, the truth is that resilience does not come naturally to a child after a traumatic experience. Instead, it is a combination of three factors that help them grow and become resilient. To support a child in building resilience, it is important to acknowledge and celebrate the milestones they have already achieved, use positive reinforcement, and practice the three key factors of resilience.

Connectedness

When a child is facing a challenging situation, it is crucial that they feel connected to the people around them. This sense of relatedness provides the child with a feeling of belonging, understanding, and security, which helps them cope with their situation. Having a nurturing adult who can provide a strong, stable, and long-lasting connection for the child to lean on can help them develop resilience. This way, they won't feel alone or isolated when experiencing difficulties.

Mastery

An important aspect of a child's development and resilience is their self-belief, which is formed during childhood. When a child succeeds in achieving a task or making a difference, their thought process changes, and their brain wiring is altered. They become more confident in their ability to reach their goals, and they become more willing to take risks, fail, and overcome obstacles.

Emotional Regulation

Trauma can affect the way the brain communicates, leading to a breakdown in communication between the left and right sides of the brain. This dysfunction can make it challenging for a child to regulate their emotions. However, therapies that focus on enhancing emotional regulation can help children learn to manage and understand their emotions better. These therapies can also help improve a child's resilience.

True resilience and growth don't mean that one is immune to challenges and difficulties. Instead, it means pushing through and persisting, no matter how difficult it may seem. The process of growth begins when a child (and even an adult) realizes that they may not be good at everything, that they may fail, and that things won't always be easy. Despite these challenges, they keep going because every failure brings a lesson and an opportunity for growth.

Encouraging the Child's Passions and Talents

Foster children who miss school or transfer frequently may miss out on assessments of their interests and talents. It's important to identify and encourage these passions to help them grow and become more resilient.

Identifying Strengths and Interests

Children are explorers. They are curious and enjoy telling stories. These natural inclinations are not just drawing pictures, playing dress up, and building with blocks, but it shows that their imagination is limitless. Children naturally gravitate toward the things they like and want to do.

Observation Is Key

Observing a child while they play is a great way to identify their strengths and interests. Take note of the things they enjoy doing and the things they're not afraid to try. You can create a checklist of skills and interests in advance and keep track of which skills the child displays. Paying close attention to the child's behavior is crucial in determining their abilities and discovering where their talents and interests lie.

Write It Down

Make sure to record any observations you make about the child's interests. Keep all your observations in one place and group them into two categories: situational, which are temporary interests that arise due to a specific activity, event, or environment, and personal interests, which are more long-term and reflective of the child's individual preferences.

Listen to What They Say

One of the best ways to identify and recognize a child's interests, passions, or strengths is to actively listen to what they are communicating to you. Children, especially younger ones, tend to be straightforward and honest when expressing themselves. Therefore, paying attention to what they are saying and how they are feeling can be extremely helpful. Additionally, observing their body language can provide valuable insights into their thoughts and emotions.

Nurture Strengths and Support Exploration

Identify your child's strengths and nurture them by allowing them to explore their interests. Encouraging them to explore helps them discover hidden talents and abilities while developing a passion for learning.

Applaud Efforts and Encourage Authenticity

Encourage your child's strengths and efforts with positive reinforcement. Teach them that it's okay to try new things and stop when they don't enjoy them. This helps them develop a growth mindset and pursue their goals without feeling stuck.

Children are natural imitators of their environments, and this is how they learn. It is crucial to teach them the importance of being themselves. Encourage them to express their opinions, even when they differ from others, and to voice their thoughts and feelings with confidence. Teaching children the value of being authentic to themselves helps them understand that they do not need to seek validation or conform to please others.

Resources and Activities for Enrichment

Enrichment activities are crucial for the growth and development of a child. They offer opportunities for exploration, nurturing of passions, and overall personal development. While schools provide some enrichment activities, it is equally important to encourage and provide these activities at home to ensure the well-rounded growth of the child.

Enrichment activities help children develop new skills, discover their interests, and cultivate a love for learning. To identify the right activities, you should consider the child's strengths and interests and then use these as a guide to explore suitable activities and resources. However, it is essential not to limit the child's exploration to their interests alone. Introduce them to new activities so they can discover new talents and interests.

Enrichment activities can come in various forms, such as creative arts, outdoor exploration, sports, debate, entrepreneurship, community service, technology, science, and engineering.

STEM projects are fantastic enrichment activities. STEM stands for Science, Technology, Engineering, and Math. It includes activities such as conducting science experiments and engineering projects like building a volcano, creating different paper airplanes to test their designs, or making a paper rocket. There are plenty of resources available that offer a wide range of ideas for STEM projects that can be easily done at home.

Building Traditions and Creating Lasting Bonds

Engaging in various activities with your foster child can help you establish a strong bond and create cherished memories. However, as we mentioned in previous sections, building family traditions and rituals is equally important in creating lasting memories and bonds with your foster child.

Family traditions and rituals should reflect the values that you want to instill in your children while promoting good family dynamics and a sense of belonging. You should take into account your child's cultural and religious background and explore ways to incorporate these holidays into your family's traditions to make them feel part of your family. Additionally, try to include them in your own family traditions and rituals.

Traditions and rituals not only make difficult transitions easier but also promote emotional regulation, teach values, provide a sense of safety, and give meaning to everyone involved. When all family members participate in traditions and rituals, as well as enrichment activities, they create memories that often leave a lasting impression. Experiences that bring joy, safety, laughter, comfort, and love are cherished and remembered fondly. Remember, sometimes, the smallest acts of love and care can create the best memories.

Ideas for Traditions

Here are some ways to help a foster child feel loved, welcomed, safe, and connected within your family.

- lunchbox notes
- family cuddle sessions or group hugs
- secret handshakes
- themed meals
- Sunday breakfasts
- adventure day
- living room campout
- yes day
- birthday king/queen (the birthday person is treated as royalty for the day)
- picnic/hiking day
- decorating the Christmas tree/making personal ornaments for the tree
- dress-up family dinner

When a foster child enters into a new home, their entire world is thrown out of balance, or perhaps it has been this way for a while. It takes a lot of time, patience, and effort to help them find stability and security again. Some aspects of their life cannot be controlled, but in terms of fostering a positive attitude, a sense of motivation, and a desire to explore and develop their skills and abilities, you can be a source of encouragement, support, and praise.

Chapter 8:

Supporting Transitions:

Reunification or Adoption

Throughout this book, we have emphasized that the main goal of foster care is reunification. In this chapter, we will discuss the complex emotions that arise during reunification and how you can prepare yourself and the child for this transition. Reunification can be bittersweet, as it marks the moment when a child returns to their birth family. However, there may be situations where the child cannot return to their birth family, and instead, they may transition to the adoption process. In this chapter, we will provide an overview of the adoption process, your role as foster parents, and the possibility of adopting the child already in your care. Transitions can be difficult, but with the proper support and preparation, you can help the child and yourself successfully navigate this process.

The Emotional Complexity of Reunification

The process of reunification can involve a mix of challenging and intricate emotions. As a foster parent, you've formed a special relationship with the child under your care, and the thought of letting go and no longer being responsible for their well-being can trigger a range of emotions. Similarly, the child may also experience a diverse set of feelings when returning to their birth family and leaving your care behind.

Understanding the Mixed Emotions

It's normal to have mixed feelings when a child you've been caring for is returned to their birth family. You may feel happy for the child to reunite with their family, but you also feel like you're losing the child. You may feel guilt, sadness, and grief. Acknowledge these emotions, understand them, and remind yourself of the end goal.

The foster care agency can offer you various resources and connect you to support groups that can help you navigate through this difficult time. Sometimes, all we require is someone to listen to us and remind us that we are not alone. Do not hesitate to take advantage of opportunities to receive assistance or ask for support. Self-care is crucial during the reunification process.

Reunification can be an emotional ride for both you and the foster child. The child may feel excited, sad, guilty, or resistant. Validate their emotions and reassure them.

The Reunification Process

The reunification process timeline is uncertain and can take weeks to years with potential setbacks. However, the overall process remains the same.

Shift in Active Roles

Once a child enters your home, you take on the role of their active caregiver. This involves taking them to school, feeding them, helping them with their schoolwork, and providing them with love and care. However, as the reunification process with their birth parents begins, a weekend visit is possible before the child is return to their birth parents. More often than not, the child leaves your care and moves back into the care of their birth parents.

As the reunification process progresses and the caseworker deems it appropriate, monitored return occurs. In this case, the child may have supervised and extended visits with their birth family, and in some cases, they may even spend a night or two a week with them.

As the caseworker becomes more confident in the birth parent's ability to provide proper care, your role as the active caregiver will gradually decrease. Over time, the caseworker will have you step back more and more as the child's active caregiver and transfer responsibilities to the birth parents. The process will come to an end when the child is officially returned to the care of their birth parents permanently.

Remain Connected and Supportive

To best support both you and the child's birth families through this transition, fostering positive relationships and maintaining regular contact, as agreed upon, is highly recommended. As a foster parent, you can engage in communication by letter or other agreed-upon means with the birth parents, facilitating mutual support. Sharing information about the child's preferences, routines, and milestones can help foster understanding and cooperation.

Establishing healthy relationships between you and the birth parents benefits everyone involved. However, it's essential to be prepared for situations where the birth families may not wish to maintain connections after the child's return to their care. While this may feel personal, it's often not the case. For birth families, interacting with you may evoke painful memories or feelings of threat, particularly if their child has formed a strong bond with you or begun to refer to you as "mommy" or "daddy."

The reunification process is undeniably challenging, marked by intense emotions and, at times, a grieving period. Yet, witnessing a child return to their birth parents is profoundly rewarding, offering reassurance that they will not be permanently separated from their family of origin.

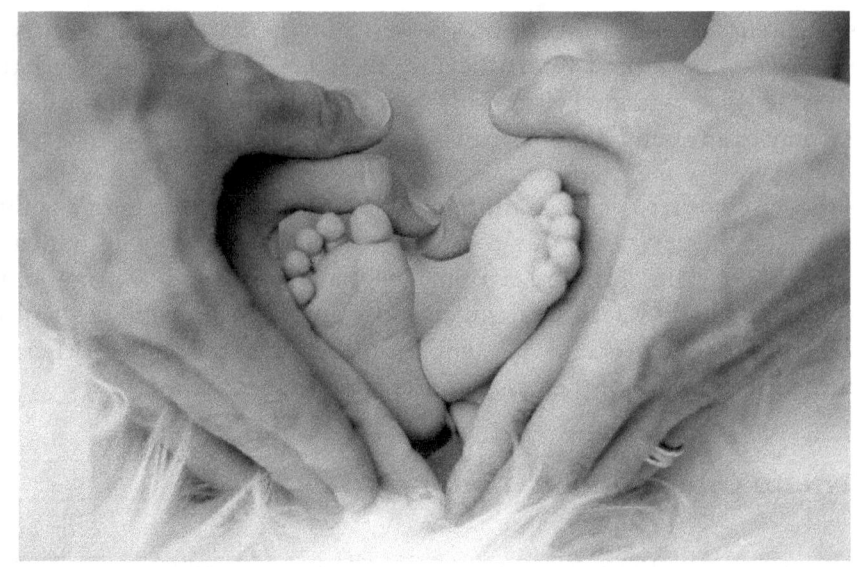

The Alternative Pathway: Adoption

When reunification with birth families is not possible, adoption becomes an option for the child. This transition evokes a mix of emotions for everyone involved. If birth families have been unable to make necessary changes for a safe environment, legal rights may be terminated by a court. In such cases, foster children may grapple with overwhelming feelings like disappointment, sadness, loneliness, or depression.

In some instances, these emotions may have already surfaced when the child entered foster care, aware of the termination of parental rights and the possibility of adoption. Regardless of the circumstances, the process of a foster child being adopted triggers a range of emotions. Foster parents may feel sadness, guilt, or hesitation in forming bonds with potential adoptive parents, yet also find joy in knowing the child will have a permanent home.

Similarly, the child will experience a mix of emotions, seeking reassurance and answers. As a foster parent, you play a crucial role in providing support and guidance through this transition, offering comfort and assurance that adoption can bring positive change.

Adoption Process

When you decided to register as a foster parent, you were required to fill out an application and go through a home study process. Similarly, prospective adoptive parents will also need to go through a home study process before they can be approved.

- After approval of adoptive parents, a caseworker matches a child to the family, similar to how they matched a foster child. Finding the right adoptive parents can be a long process due to careful consideration.

- The caseworker will work with you to establish visits between the child and adoptive parents, and once they are familiar with each other, the child will be placed with the adoptive parents.

- Before adoptive parents can file a petition for adoption, a waiting period is provided to allow both the parents and child to adjust to their new family situation. Once the waiting period is over, the adoptive parents are free to file their petition for adoption.

- During a court hearing, a judge signs the final adoption decree in the presence of the family.

If you have a child in your care and want to adopt them, the adoption process is simpler since the home study has been conducted, and the child is already with you. However, additional interviews may occur to ensure this is the right choice for you and the child.

Preparing the Child for Change

Preparing a child for reunification or adoption can be challenging, but consistency, support, and active listening can help make the transition easier.

Reunification Transition

When you're having talks about reunifying with a child, it's important to approach them with positivity, excitement, and transparency. If you show any doubt or hesitation, the child may pick up on it from your non-verbal cues. So, it's essential to be mindful of your tone, facial expressions, and word choices during these discussions.

- Have a private conversation with them, explain what's happening, and be transparent about the process.

- Be patient and give them time to process. Offer to continue the conversation later or stay with them until they're ready. Avoid leaving unless they've explicitly said they need to be alone.

- Answer any questions they may have and provide reassurance wherever possible. Listen to what they are saying and be attentive to any concerns they might express. Acknowledge and validate their emotions and concerns. Let them know that it is completely normal to have mixed emotions and feel uncertain.

- Let them know that you will always be there for them, and they can call or message you whenever they want. Reassure them that it is good to return to their birth parents and that you are happy for them. Tell them that you love them and want the best for them.

Stay consistent and avoid making too many changes during the transition process. Be available to the child, offer support, and maintain normalcy. This will provide them with a sense of security and stability during the transition.

Adoption Transition

Your tone, choice of words, and verbal cues are crucial when explaining the situation to the child and helping them understand what's happening.

How to approach this transition:
- Have a private conversation with them and share exciting details about the adoptive parents to make the child feel more welcome to the idea.

- Explain the process step-by-step to them.

- In cases where you choose not to adopt the foster child. Assure them that being adopted by another family doesn't mean you don't love them or don't want them around. Let them know that you love them and this is an exciting opportunity for them.

- Give them time to process and be near unless instructed otherwise.

- Answer their questions and listen to their concerns. Where possible, share details about the adoptive family so that things can feel more real for them and they can consider all that you've told them.

When adopting a child in your care, it's important to have a private conversation with them first. Although announcing the adoption on social media may seem heartwarming, it could make the child feel pressured to react or behave in a certain way.

As a foster parent, it would be beneficial for all parties involved if you maintain open and honest communication with the adoptive parents and provide them with support. Sharing information such as the history, routines, likes, and dislikes of the child can help the adoptive parents be better prepared. You can also share photos and memories with them, which will help them get to know the child better. Additionally, it would be helpful to ask the adoptive parents to provide information and pictures of themselves so that you can prepare the child before they officially meet the adoptive parents.

Reuniting a child with their birth parents or finding their forever home can be emotional. Honest conversations and self-care are important for both the child and you.

Chapter 9:

Self-Care for Foster Parents:

Avoiding Burnout

As a foster parent or caregiver, you are constantly giving your time, energy, and emotional capacity to the person you are caring for. This can be especially challenging when caring for a child who has experienced trauma and can easily drain you. To maintain your well-being, it is essential to practice self-care and build resilience. Having a supportive system in place can also be helpful during difficult times.

The Importance of Self-Care and Resilience

As a foster parent, it is important to be aware that children in your care may project their hurt onto you and blame you for their feelings of loss and despair. You may have tried to prepare yourself by learning about a child's history before they entered your home, but sometimes, they might share or say something that reveals a trauma that was previously unknown. Similarly, you may assume that their behavior will be less challenging, but it turns out to be the opposite. Therefore, it is crucial that you learn to build resilience and practice self-care so that when things become overwhelming and rough, you have ways to refill your cup and a support system to lean on until you have recharged yourself.

It is often said that you cannot pour from an empty cup, and this is especially true for foster parents. When your cup is empty, you may not be able to provide effective care to the children in your charge. Your energy is sapped, your mood is low, and you may feel overwhelmed and the need to escape it all, even for just an hour. It is natural to feel these things, and it is your body's way of telling you that you need to care for yourself.

Barriers to Good Self-Care

As a foster parent, you may feel like you need to be a superhero who can do it all, but it's important to remember that you're human. Asking for help and relying on support can help you build resilience and provide better care for your foster child.

Some barriers that might prevent you from reaching out to your support network or caring for yourself are:

- If you are someone who naturally takes care of others, it might be uncomfortable for you to be the one receiving care and attention. However, it's important to remember that it's okay to take care of yourself and allow others to care for you. This doesn't make you weak or needy because everyone needs support at some point in their lives. Remember that you are human, and you deserve to be taken care of just as much as you take care of others.

- Don't try to be everything for everyone all the time. It's okay to prioritize and take care of yourself. Be available when it matters most, especially for the people who matter most, like your foster child. Don't stress yourself too thin to the point of not being fully present when it matters.

- Perhaps you think that foster parents should be able to handle everything without any support or help, as it was their choice to become foster parents. However, this is not true. Even the most successful and composed foster parents know when to ask for help, when to lean on the people around them, and that it's okay to struggle at times.

- Many of us were told as children that we should be content with what we have because others have it worse. Although this remark was intended to be innocent, it may have also caused some of us to feel guilty. We feel guilty when our struggles and trauma do not compare to others, and we downplay our own difficulties. We neglect to acknowledge the challenges we face because we think that they could be worse. However, the truth is that your struggles are significant to you. So, when you are struggling, do not listen to those feelings of guilt. Instead, recognize that you are only human, and it is okay to need help and support.

Recognizing Burnout

Caring for a traumatized child can be emotionally taxing. Trauma is contagious; when exposed to others' trauma, you may experience secondary trauma. Vicarious trauma (also known as secondary trauma) is when you experience the effects of trauma when hearing another's first-hand accounts of trauma (Matejko, 2022). Vicarious trauma can be linked to burnout and compassion fatigue, which is why we're discussing it. Most foster care children experience trauma, which can negatively impact you.

Managing busy commitments and schedules can easily become overwhelming, especially when you are dealing with the emotional toll of caring for foster children. It's common to feel ineffective and struggle to continue serving as a foster parent when you're at the brink of burnout or have already crossed it. Recognizing the signs of burnout early can help you find the support you need before it becomes too much to handle. Some of the signs to look out for are:

- disrupted sleeping patterns
- intrusive thoughts
- anxiety
- feeling overwhelmed with simple tasks
- having an intense reaction to small things
- short temper
- extreme sadness or constant crying
- isolating or withdrawing socially
- being forgetful or struggling to form sentences or even think of words

Burnout can occur during various stages of fostering, such as when you receive your first placement, when your first placement leaves, when the child is struggling, when they are reunited with their parents or adopted, when undisclosed trauma is revealed, when a new placement arrives, but you are still grieving the previous placement, or when a significant event happens in your family like a death, illness, loss of a pet, job, or an older child moving out. It is crucial to be mindful of the signs of burnout and learn what triggers them. This will help you find coping strategies that work for you and aid in your recovery from burnout.

Compassion Fatigue

Compassion fatigue is a state of exhaustion that often affects caregivers exposed to prolonged stress and trauma. It leads to a decrease in compassion capacity, emotional drain, feelings of being overwhelmed, decreased empathy, cynicism, irritability, fatigue, and hopelessness.

Just like your emotional and physical capacity, your compassion cup also needs refilling. Whether it's due to secondary trauma, burnout, compassion fatigue, or just general feelings of things being tough, it's important to prioritize self-care. Learn to ask for help, and lean on those around you when you need it.

Activities and Rituals for Self-Care

Self-care means taking care of your physical and mental well-being. Find activities that work for you and do them daily, weekly, and monthly.

Here are some ideas for you to consider incorporating into your self-care practices:

- Zone out by watching a movie, reading a book, or listening to music.

- Don't multitask, but be present in every moment.

- Pay attention to your body's signals that it needs you to slow down.

- Practice mindfulness, whether by keeping a journal or meditating.

- Go for a walk or exercise.

- Do something creative—paint, draw, or dance.

- Have a glass of wine on a Friday night.

- Have an uninterrupted bath.

- Bake something that smells good.

- Spend time with friends.

- Take a vacation.

- Treat yourself to something tasty, luxurious, or just your favorite meal.

- Go to church or pray.

- Get a massage.

- Attend support groups or therapy sessions.

- Set healthy boundaries.

- Spend some quality family time.

Practicing self-care can help reduce anxiety and depression, lessen stress, improve focus and happiness, and lower the risk of stroke and heart disease.

Building a Support System

Remember to take care of yourself and surround yourself with a support system that you can rely on. It's important to recognize that caring for a child who has experienced trauma and has challenging behaviors can be overwhelming. Add to this that you're taking care of another person's child and this can all become a bit overwhelming. Building a support system is essential to prevent burnout, refill your cup, and get through tough times.

In foster care, there are many resources and information available to help you navigate the rules and regulations that may feel confusing. These resources include guidance, services, and programs that can help you acquire skills to manage challenging situations. Don't forget that your caseworker is a valuable source of information and can guide you toward a support group for foster parents.

Support groups and online communities can be a great help when you feel like you're alone in your experiences. Knowing that others are going through similar struggles can be comforting during difficult times. Sometimes, sharing your experiences and being heard is all you need to find guidance and support. Additionally, support groups can help you connect with other foster families who might be able to offer respite care.

Respite care is a service that is offered to foster parents who need a break for a few hours, a night, or even a weekend. During respite care, a foster family takes in your foster children for a short period, allowing you to take a break. You can also consider respite care if you need some time to recover from the grief of your first placement, whether your foster child has been reunified with their parents or has been adopted.

Identify **friends and family** members who can offer emotional support for you when needed. Having someone to listen to you and knowing they are just a phone call away can make a significant difference in building your resilience. Sometimes, all you need is a pep talk and a good laugh with a loved one. Never underestimate the importance of relying on friends and family during your times of difficulty, even when it's hard to ask for help.

Finally, there may be times when you require additional **professional assistance** to help you navigate through challenging situations. This may include counseling services or therapy sessions for either yourself or your child, educational support to help you improve, or healthcare professionals who can educate you on the best ways to care for a child with special needs and ensure that they receive the care and support they require.

Remember, it's okay to ask for help. It's okay to struggle. And it's okay to take care of yourself. Being a caregiver is fulfilling, but it has its ups and downs. What matters is how you handle the difficult times. You become more resilient when you learn to care for yourself, ask for help, and seek support. Knowing your weaknesses and how to overcome them will make you strong enough to face any challenge that comes your way.

Chapter 10:

Continuing the Journey: Lifelong Learning and Advocacy

As a foster parent, you are on a continuous journey of learning, improving, and developing skills. The training you receive to become a foster parent is just the beginning. The experiences and learning opportunities don't stop or slow down after your first foster child placement. In fact, it's quite the opposite. Caregiving changes as new techniques, treatments, and methods are discovered to help foster children with trauma and special needs. This chapter is dedicated to helping you continue your journey as a foster parent. We will explore what your future goals might be and what to do when you need to advocate loudly for the child in your care.

Continuous Training Opportunities and Their Importance

As a prospective foster parent, you need to attend a set number of training sessions during the approval phase to acquire the necessary skills for your foster parent journey. Apart from the basic training, several agencies provide additional training sessions throughout the year to help you develop more valuable skills. It's important to note that some states may require you to accumulate a specific number of training hours within a year to ensure that you are up-to-date with all the training and policy and legislative changes that may impact you or the child in your care.

Some of the training that agencies may provide are:

- attachment disorder awareness training

- trauma-informed care

- grief and transition training

- hyper-vigilance, dissociation, ADHD, and other conduct disorders

- PTSD, or Complex PTSD

- care for sexually abused children

- addiction and self-harm care

- disability awareness

- gang culture and crime awareness

It's important for foster parents to receive proper training to help them deal with the challenges of fostering. Some agencies offer more in-depth training sessions that focus on helping foster parents cope with the grief that comes with having their first placement reunite with their birth family or become adopted. They also offer self-care sessions aimed at helping foster parents develop healthy coping skills and resilience.

You can speak to your foster care agency, social worker, or state agencies to see if there are any upcoming learning opportunities that you can attend. Most training sessions have become hybrid since COVID, which allows you to attend sessions from the comfort of your home if you are unable to travel.

The more skills and knowledge you have, the better equipped you will be to anticipate and handle each new placement that comes into your care. However, your learning doesn't have to start and end with agency training sessions. If you desire, you can reach out to local colleges and see if they offer short courses on the skills you want to develop. Alternatively, you can search for credible online resources, such as blog posts or videos, that can teach you valuable skills.

Advocating for Foster Children

Advocacy is a powerful tool for bringing about change where it is needed. As a foster parent, it is crucial that you keep yourself updated on the child's progress in school, medical appointments, and therapy sessions, and attend all meetings with anyone involved in the child's life, such as parents, doctors, specialists, etc. Additionally, you should be familiar with the child's case plan, which is a file containing their goals, needs, and the services they require. This will help you ensure that they are getting the necessary support and services.

With the information and experiences you have with the child, you can advocate for them, ensuring that their best interests are considered during all decision-making processes. If you think your rights as a foster parent or the child's rights are being violated, or if the decisions being made are not serving the child, do not be afraid to speak up.

Remember that you are the eyes and ears of the foster child, the person who sees them struggling and notices the challenges they are facing. You can actively be the voice for that child, so speak up when you need to.

Possible Challenging When Advocating

It's important to keep in mind that while the social worker of a foster child always has the child's best interest at heart, disagreements can arise, and people may have different perspectives on how to best move forward for the child. It's important to avoid getting on the social worker's bad side, especially since they have the power to remove the child from your care. However, you should be aware that you have the right to be heard, and your concerns about the child and their well-being matter and should be advocated for.

It's important to be aware that filing a complaint against a social worker or disagreeing with them can put you in a difficult position. You may find it challenging to advocate for the child or yourself if you end up in such a situation. Therefore, it's crucial to familiarize yourself with the state and local policies and regulations that govern your rights and ability to advocate for the child.

Below are a few ways to ensure that you and the social worker share the same goals and to be heard when you can't reach an agreement.

Open Communication

It is important to remember that social workers are responsible for managing multiple children at any given time. When decisions are made that do not seem right for a child, it is important to communicate with the social worker and ask why such decisions were made. At times, social workers may be bound by legal requirements or court orders and may not have made the decision themselves. In other cases, they may not have had enough information to make better decisions.

Therefore, it is essential that you and the social worker maintain open communication with each other. They may not be aware of the challenges you or the child are facing, or that the child's needs have changed. By keeping the social worker informed, you are providing them with all the necessary information to make informed decisions that positively impact the child.

Remember, advocating for the child in your care is crucial. Simply sharing your perspective can have a significant impact on the direction of decision-making.

Make Your Concerns Heard

If you find that your attempts to communicate with a social worker about a child's well-being are not producing any results, you can take the next step by contacting the social worker's supervisor. It is understandable to feel frustrated, but it's important to approach the supervisor calmly and professionally. Provide them with relevant background information and any other important details that they may not be aware of.

Avoid blaming the social worker unless it is absolutely necessary. During the conversation with the supervisor, make it clear what is happening presently, what changes you would like to see, and why those changes are necessary.

If the supervisor is unable to understand, agree, or have the authority to make the necessary changes, you may need to escalate the situation to a higher authority, such as a manager. Repeat the same process with the manager and continue to escalate the situation until your concerns are addressed.

Quality Control Team or Foster Parent Association

Depending on the agency, there may be a team or individual responsible for quality control or policy control. This person is responsible for addressing complaints within the agency and can help you clarify rules and procedures, as well as guide you through the next steps in the process.

In some states, Foster Parent Associations are available to assist you by clarifying rules and procedures and acting as a support person during meetings. This can be extremely helpful, as they can act as a buffer between you and the agency during meetings, and they can also serve as witnesses.

If this service is not available to you, don't hesitate to bring another professional, family member, or foster parent with you to these meetings to act as a witness. If they possess expertise, they can also provide guidance for you.

Remember, you are advocating for the child in your care, but the changes you are advocating for may make a world of difference for another foster family, child, or even others. So, don't be afraid to let your voice and concerns be heard.

Looking Beyond: Becoming a Mentor for New Foster Parents

Foster parenting is a rewarding experience that can lead to other opportunities to make a difference in the lives of children in need. If you have experience as a foster parent, you can use your skills and knowledge to mentor new foster parents. This can help to increase retention of foster parents, reduce transitions for foster children, and prevent burnout.

When new foster parents feel overwhelmed, it can be helpful for them to talk to someone who has been through the same experiences. They may not feel comfortable sharing their concerns with a caseworker, but they can confide in a mentor who understands their situation and can provide emotional support.

Mentoring is a two-way street that benefits both the mentor and the mentee. New foster parents can rely on their mentor for advice, guidance, and support during difficult times. The mentor, in turn, can develop a close relationship with the new foster parents, gain mutual support, and learn from a fresh perspective.

Qualities of a Mentor

Mentors should possess experience, knowledge, and personal qualities to be effective. Personal qualities include being a good listener, non-judgmental, easy-going, approachable, and calm during challenges.

A good mentor must be available for those they are mentoring, providing guidance, advice, and support to new foster parents. This accessibility helps mentors build a reliable support network while allowing foster parents to gain confidence in their caregiving skills.

Mentoring is a valuable support mechanism within the foster care system. While social workers offer resources and insights, mentoring provides a deeper learning experience that benefits both parties.

Ultimately, the decision to become a mentor and help other foster parents is up to you. By doing so, you can help others find their footing and provide loving homes for the children who come into their lives.

As a foster parent, your journey isn't limited to the duration of a placement. It's a continuous journey that presents new opportunities even when you don't have a child in your home. To perform your best, you need the right skills and tools, which you can acquire only by constantly striving to be a lifelong learner. Whether it's attending specialized training sessions, learning to advocate for yourself and the child, or aiming to become a mentor, this journey is rewarding and fulfilling.

Conclusion

Embarking on this journey of becoming a foster parent means taking the road less traveled. This road may be windy and have obstacles, but it's also filled with the warmth of joy, transformation, and learning. As we reach the end of this book, it's crucial to take a moment to pause, reflect, and absorb the insights you have gained from each chapter.

The core belief of foster care is that every child deserves to be loved, to have a stable and nurturing environment, and to be cared for. This foundational concept, discussed in the initial chapters, highlights the crucial role that foster parents play in providing safe havens for children who have experienced trauma through no fault of their own. Understanding the complexities of the system and recognizing the behaviors resulting from trauma can be challenging, but the impact of this work is profound.

As a foster parent, you will come to realize that each child who enters your home has a unique story to tell. Their challenges, successes, memories, dreams, laughter, and tears all make up a beautiful picture of their life so far. By understanding the concepts of attachment and trauma, you will learn about the profound impact that traumatic experiences can have on a child. However, you will also come to realize that love and patience can have a transformative effect on these children. This book emphasizes that while past experiences may leave scars, the future is full of limitless possibilities for happiness, growth, and healing.

Fostering is not a journey that one takes alone, but rather, it is a journey that is shared with others. Foster parents work closely with caseworkers and the remainder of the support team and recognize the vital role that birth families play in the process. They are at the heart of these relationships and navigate them with care, respect, and mutual understanding.

Throughout these chapters, you have gained insight into the significance of being a guardian for a child's memories, life goals, and aspirations.

You have learned the importance of acknowledging their small achievements and providing support to help them reach significant milestones. Equipping a child with essential skills is vital in preparing them for a successful future.

Transitions can be the most challenging part of the journey. When a placement ends, or a child is reunited with their birth parents or adopted, it can feel like you've lost someone dear. It's normal to grieve during such transitions. However, even though grief is natural, self-care is crucial, both during these transitions and while taking care of a child with trauma. You can only give what you have, so it's important to take regular care of yourself and build resilience.

This book offers guidance, insights, and strategies, but at its core, it's about the heart. The heart that opens its doors to a child in need, the heart that remains resilient through challenges, and the heart that celebrates small victories, cherishes laughter and provides solace during the storms.

If there's one takeaway, let it be this: **Fostering is more than just providing a temporary home. It's about shaping futures, building connections, and anchoring children in the belief that they deserve unconditional love and a bright future.**

As you embark on your journey of fostering, let it be an experience that fills your heart with hope, warmth, and a love that transforms lives. Your journey has the power to illuminate countless futures, touch the hearts of many, and create an endless stream of stories that will inspire and uplift those around you. May your journey be one of self-discovery, compassion, and a deep sense of purpose as you make a difference in the lives of those around you.

Glossary

Abuse: Treat a child or person with cruelty or violence, which can be emotional, sexual, or physical.

Adoption: Process in which a child legally becomes a member of their adoptive family.

Aging out: A term that refers to a foster child who has turned 18 and is no longer part of the foster care system—they are deemed adults and capable of being responsible for their own well-being.

Burnout: A mental state where a person feels an overwhelming exhaustion due to prolonged exposure to stressors in their jobs.

Compassion fatigue: A fatigue that's experienced in caregivers whose compassion toward those they care for becomes affected, and they feel worn down and ineffective in their duties. Their cups are running empty.

CPS: Acronym for child protective services.

Group home: A homelike facility that provides care to a group of foster children.

Home study: Process in which foster parents and adoptive parents are vetted to ensure they can provide a loving and caring home to a child. Includes various aspects of information gathering.

IEP: Acronym for individualized educational plan. This plan is created for public students who have been identified as having a learning or thinking disability that requires specialized educational goals and resources.

Neglect: Failure to provide proper care to a child or person.

PTSD: Acronym for post-traumatic stress disorder, a disorder that some foster children may suffer from due to prolonged abuse or neglect.

Respite care: Care service offered to foster parents when they need a few hours, a night, or a weekend to themselves—this service takes in the foster child for a short period.

Reunification: Process where a foster child is reunited with their birth or previous caregivers.

SEN: Acronym for special education needs. This refers to students who require specialized educational resources and services.

STEM: Acronym for science, technology, engineering, and mathematics.

Subsidy: A sum of money granted by the state to assist foster parents in caring for a foster child's needs.

TMC: Acronym for temporary managing conservatorship.

References

Big Fish Local. (2021, November 25). *Foster facts: How long can you foster a child?* Benchmark Family Services Therapeutic Foster Care. https://benchmarkfamilyservices.org/foster-facts-how-long-can-you-foster-a-child/#:~:text=Other%20times%20a%20child%20may

Hamblen, J., & Barnett, E. (2023). *PTSD in children and adolescents*. National Center for PTSD. https://www.ptsd.va.gov/professional/treat/specific/ptsd_child_teens.asp

Matejko, S. (2022, March 10). *Vicarious trauma: Causes, symptoms, and how to cope* (M. Boland PhD, Ed.). Psych Central. https://psychcentral.com/health/vicarious-trauma#symptoms

National Foster Youth Institution. (2023). Fifty-one *useful aging out of foster care statistics*. Nfyi.org; National Foster Youth Institute. https://nfyi.org/51-useful-aging-out-of-foster-care-statistics-social-race-media/

The Annie E. Casey Foundation. (2022, May 20). *What is foster care?* The Annie E. Casey Foundation. https://www.aecf.org/blog/what-is-foster-care

Image References

Abdelghaffar, M. (2018). Toddler with red Adidas sweat shirt [Image]. In *Pexels*. https://www.pexels.com/photo/toddler-with-red-adidas-sweat-shirt-783941/

Altmann, G. (2015). Traffic sign training [Image]. In *Pixabay*. https://pixabay.com/photos/traffic-signs-place-name-sign-798175/

Altmann, G. (2016). Family children togetherness [Image]. In *Pixabay*. https://pixabay.com/illustrations/family-children-togetherness-1466262/

Budy, A. (2019). Cry sadness child [Image]. In *Pixabay*. https://pixabay.com/vectors/cry-sadness-child-alone-emotion-4250450/

Catatanbelajar. (2022). Icon logo medical [Image]. In *Pixabay*. https://pixabay.com/illustrations/icon-logo-medical-health-7042847/

CottonBro Studio. (2020). Two girls playing with stuffed animals [Image]. In *Pexels*. https://www.pexels.com/photo/photo-of-two-girls-playing-with-stuffed-animals-3662839/

Hassan, M. (2018). Child protection services [Image]. In *Pixabay*. https://pixabay.com/vectors/child-protection-services-cps-3583417/

Hassan, M. (2019). Audit tax inspection [Image]. In *Pixabay*. https://pixabay.com/illustrations/audit-tax-inspection-auditor-3929140/

Hassan, M. (2022). Brain psychology autism [Image]. In *Pixabay*. https://pixabay.com/vectors/brain-psychology-autism-awareness-7512388/

Jan. (2017). House icon symbol [Image]. In *Pixabay*. https://pixabay.com/vectors/house-icon-symbol-architecture-2492054/

Krukau, Y. (n.d.). Happy children playing with colorful plastic balls [Image]. In *Pexels*. https://www.pexels.com/photo/happy-children-playing-with-colorful-plastic-balls-8613149/

Linforth, P. (2017). Mentoring business success [Image]. In *Pixabay*. https://pixabay.com/photos/mentoring-business-success-mentor-2738524/

Monstera Production. (2020). Young girls exploring together [Image]. In *Pexels*. https://www.pexels.com/photo/photo-of-young-girl-exploring-together-5063444/

Pixabay. (n.d.). Two girls walking on brown bridge [Image]. In *Pexels*. https://www.pexels.com/photo/2-girl-walking-on-brown-bridge-during-daytime-50581/

Ovcharenko, N. (2017). Group therapy counseling [Image]. In *Pixabay*. https://pixabay.com/illustrations/group-therapy-counseling-health-2351896/

Robert Fotograf. (2016). Welcome to our home plate [Image]. In *Pixabay*. https://pixabay.com/photos/welcome-to-our-home-welcome-plate-1205888/

Tarekegn, E. (2019). Boy and girl sitting on floor outdoor [Image]. In *Pexels*. https://www.pexels.com/photo/boy-and-girl-sitting-on-floor-outdoor-2180141/

User 5921373. (2017). Infant feet father [Image]. In *Pixabay*. https://pixabay.com/photos/infant-feet-father-mother-2717347/

Wokandapix. (2013). Education school [Image]. In *Pixabay*. https://pixabay.com/photos/education-school-back-to-school-908512/

Wokandapix. (2020). Self care [Image]. In *Pixabay*. https://pixabay.com/photos/self-care-self-care-self-reliance-4899284/

www.ingramcontent.com/pod-product-compliance
Lightning Source LLC
Chambersburg PA
CBHW071235090426
42736CB00014B/3093